LAUGH AGAIN WITH
ANDY CAPP

© 1976 Mirror Group Newspapers Ltd.
Published by Mirror Group Books,
79 Camden Road, London, NW1 9NT.
Printed and bound in England by
Hazell Watson & Viney Ltd,
Aylesbury, Bucks.

ISBN 0 85939 069 1

A MIRROR GROUP BOOK

laugh again with

ANDY CAPP

No. 16

CARTOONS BY REG SMYTHE

1

2

3

4

1

2

3

4

3

4

1

2

1

2

3

4

1

2

1

2

3

4

THANKS F' THE LOVELY PAIR O' SOCKS YER SENT ME FOR MY BIRTHDAY, RUBY

OH, THAT'S NOTHIN' TO THANK ME FOR, ANDY—

THAT'S WHAT *I* THOUGHT, BUT FLORRIE SAID I 'AD TO

3

C'MON, MAKE UP YER MIND — SHOULD YER OR SHOULD YER NOT TELL FLORRIE —??

4

1

2